History of Keoua Kalanikupuapa-i-kalani-nui

History of Keoua Kalanikupuapa-i-kalani-nui

Father of Hawaii Kings

Elizabeth Keka'aniau
La'anui Pratt

MINT EDITIONS

History of Keoua Kalanikupuapa-i-kalani-nui: Father of Hawaii Kings was first published in 1920.

This edition published by Mint Editions 2021.

ISBN 9781513299549 | E-ISBN 9781513223865

Published by Mint Editions®

MINT
EDITIONS

minteditionbooks.com

Publishing Director: Jennifer Newens
Design & Production: Rachel Lopez Metzger
Project Manager: Micaela Clark
Typesetting: Westchester Publishing Services

Contents

EDITOR'S NOTE

This little book contains many interesting sidelights on Hawaiian history. Its appearance is happily timed with the celebration this year of the centennial of the arrival of the American missionaries, one of whose notable achievements is herein appreciatively related in the account of the establishment of the Royal School. The conversion of the subject matter from family legendary lore to literary form has been a painstaking task of several years on the part of the venerable author, a high chiefess descended from the distinguished "father of kings," whose name forms the title of the work. High Chiefess Kekaaniau Pratt had reached the age of eighty-five years when she completed the writing of "Keoua," herewith submitted to the public as a contribution to Hawaiian history, as well as a fond tribute to her renowned ancestors.

DANIEL LOGAN

Preface

In compliance with the wishes of a great many who are still unacquainted with the history of that famous chieftain known in his time and during the reign of King Kaleiopuu his half-brother, over the Island of Hawaii, as Keoua-nui, or Kalanikupuapaikalani-nui-Keoua, I shall herewith endeavor to give a meager narration of incidents in the life of that personage, together with brief memoirs of the illustrious Kamehameha dynasty, also of collateral branches of the Keoua line. It will be a record of some leading events and important sayings in the lives of those great Hawaiians of the periods immediately preceding and following the advent of foreigners into these beautiful isles of the North Pacific. These annals have been handed down from generation to generation by members of our family, as well as by genealogists and retainers, whose duty it was to preserve the history, meles and tabus of their aliis (chiefs). Modern genealogists of our own time such as Kamakau, Unauna, Fornander and others became apt scholars of the traditions and knowledge transmitted to them.

E. K. P.
Honolulu, January 22, 1920

Part I

Keoua Kalanikupuapaikalani-Nui, styled Keoua-nui, was the son of Keeaumoku-nui, second son of Keaweikekahialiiokamoku, King of Hawaii, by his second wife, Princess Kalanikauleleieiwi, granddaughter of Iwikauikaua (whose celebrated kapu was the torchlight burnt at midday) and daughter of the high chiefess Keakealani-wahine. Keoua's mother was Kamakaimoku, of the renowned family of chiefs of Kau, the I's.

This child Keoua was reared carefully with the utmost dignity due to his birth, for his father was a "Pio," which was considered among royalties as the highest rank in the realm. The blood running in his veins had come from Liloa and Umi in a direct line both on the father's and mother's side, connecting also with the royal families of Maui, Oahu and Kauai.

Keeaumokunui had an only sister, younger than he, named Kekela-nui, who, as she grew up, was sought after by many beaux, all anxious to marry into the Keawe line. Among her crowd of suitors a young chief named Haae was the favored one to win her heart and hand. Their union was blessed with a daughter whom they named Kekuiapoiwa the Second. At this time Keoua was still a child and the idea soon occurred, as was natural, to the parents of the prince and of the princess that they should be betrothed, and the ceremony to that end was carried out with due pomp by court and people. Yet this proved to be one of those instances where the "best laid schemes" go astray, as will later be seen.

Comely of person and gracious to all he met, Keoua as he verged toward manhood became an attractive personage. While yet awaiting the fulfilment of the plighted troth of his childhood, rumors of events in Maui royal circles were wafted across the waters of Alenuihaha channel which stirred his ambition. They were of the two beautiful daughters of Kalahumoku and his wife Kalani Kaumehameha. Kalahumoku was the reigning high chief of all Hana including also the districts of Kipahulu and Kaupo, whose decease had just taken place, his eldest daughter Kahikikala assuming the right of successorship in governing his people. Kalahumoku was a lineal descendant of Loe, the great progenitor of Maui's chiefdom, the Piilanis, Kamalalawalu and others, and of the Hana aliis as well.

This family possessed a wonderful tabu entirely different from, and never known to exist among, any of the other chief families of the Hawaiian group. It was styled "Ka Poo hoolewa i ka La," and inherited from Kaakaualaninui, the grandmother of Kalahumoku. It signified the laying of the head toward the sun's position in the heavens from its rising unto its setting. Days for the observance of this tabu were strictly kept. The only time for recreation during the tabu must be taken from between the setting of the luminary and the dawn of a new day.

Upon the arrival of the news just mentioned from Maui Keoua showed great restlessness and anxiety, so much so that his father beseeched him to make known his wishes. Keoua answered: "I desire to visit the court of the two young princesses of Hana, to take to wife one of them, for great is my ambition to obtain that most wonderful of all tabus, so as to hand it down to my posterity forever."

His father assented to this and preparations were immediately made to carry out the wish of the young prince. Followers, retainers and kahunas formed an imposing retinue for Prince Keoua and at dawn of a fine morning the expedition sailed away so as to reach the opposite shore of Muoleilani by noon. With the sea calm and quiet everything portended a welcome from his selected hostesses. When the fleet was sighted by the kamaainas on the Hana shore great surprise was shown on every countenance. Heralds were sent to the abode of the princesses to announce that a royal visitor was about to land. Emissaries were quickly despatched to the landing to welcome the prince and his followers and invite them to the royal abode, where Kahikikala and her sister Kalanilehua would be ready to receive them.

Upon the arrival of Keoua a truly royal greeting was exchanged between the three chiefly scions, while an equally cordial pledging of friendship took place between those accompanying the prince and those attending on the princesses. Soon it was noticed that Keoua's attention was more devoted to Kalanilehua than to her elder and regnant sister whom she distinctly outrivaled in beauty. It was said of Kalanilehua that her complexion was like the ohia blossom, from which in fact her name was derived. She was indeed most prepossessing in appearance, so that no young knight meeting her could escape being smitten by her charms.

That Keoua should have failed to conceal his preference, however, did not make any difference of feeling in Kahikikala's heart toward Kalanilehua, for not only was there great affection between the sisters but the elder held a motherly love for the younger. So matters stood until Keoua's kahuna deemed it his duty to give warning counsel to his lord, which he did in this manner:

"My Alii, you have come to the land where the sun is never seen setting in the western horizon, as the high peaks of Mauna Kauwiki obstructed the view. Therefore the aliis of Hana are called 'Na Lii oi ka La Kau;' while you have the title and distinction of the Alii of the Rising Sun—'I ka Hikina i Haehae.' Your purpose in coming here was to get a legal inheritance which you greatly coveted for yourself and your successors, that of the far-famed tabu, 'Ka Poo Hoolewa i ka La,' of which Kahikikala is the only rightful possessor, as she is the Alii Aimoku, as long as she lives, of all this country and people.

"Therefore make amends for your past indifference and lack of courtesy, and seek Kahikikala's forgiveness and respect. Besides, she being the elder-born, her progeny will always take precedence of seniority by birth."

Keoua rose to his feet and said: "I have done wrong and I shall try to make reparation for my past heedless infatuation."

Now Kalanilehua was well versed respecting her position as the only Hooilina or successor to her sister so long as her sister remained single, as well as conscious that all the honors should be paid to her sister, and aware of the duty of abiding by the monarchical law that required respect and kindness toward all royal visitors at the court. Therefore she permitted Keoua's behavior toward herself to grow no warmer, but not alone for that reason but because her heart had been already captured by a chief to the manor born—"o ka aina"—Ua Lanihaahaa, who claimed descent from the noble family of Elani. It was as if a flood of sunshine had come over her, leaving her in her full glory, free and happy.

In the meantime events were taking a different course in Kahikikala's life. Keoua was anxious for the culmination of the grand desire of his heart through the ceremony of the "Hoao." Accordingly all the subjects dwelling in Hana, Kipahulu and Kaupo were summoned for the grand hookupu and hearing of the proclamation of the "Hoao" of Keoua and Kahikikala. Feasting, dancing and merry-making in turn expressed general happiness and rejoicing until it was time for the people to return to their homes.

Weeks extended into months with Keoua happy and contented in his new home. Places of interest, including the sublime extinct crater of Haleakala, were visited by himself and retinue. To the "house of the rising sun," as the name of the vast mountain signifies, the distinguished expedition was accompanied by the best-informed guides and persons versed in the old folklore and legends of the weird region. On the fourth day they emerged from the interior of the crater through the Kaupo Pass. At the exit the vast multitude was met by the folks of that district with a well-prepared feast in honor of the alii and his party. Thence the royal excursion was continued to one of Kahikikala's homes at Kaupo, for a rest of a few days before facing the rugged trails of Kipahulu, a district noted for its precipitous cliffs and deep ravines. Upon this final stage of the return journey, Keoua, according to custom, was carried upon the backs of his sturdy lieges, one relieving another as necessary.

During all this time events at home were in a lively turn, for the people of Kipahulu and Kaupo were eager to have carried out that which they required, namely, that one of the sisters should make a resident court at Kipahulu, and they looked to Kalanilehua to gratify their longings. So the day was set that the Hoao of Kalanilehua and her devoted lover should be solemnized, it being arranged so as to take place as soon as Keoua reached home.

The repetition of the sacred ceremony was carried out, being as bright and joyous as the nuptials of Kahikikala and Keoua's had been. The day of departure for the royal couple was one of sorrow for the two sisters. Multitudes of people escorted the pair to their new home, borne on covered palanquins carried on men's shoulders.

The next event for grand celebration was the birth of Keoua's son and firstborn, who was deemed "Ka Keiki o Kona wa Heuole," which means the offspring of his beardless youth. The child was named Kalokuokamaile. Of course this brought many from other courts far and near, including people of Maui. Their rejoicings seemed to know no bounds. Kahikikala spared nothing in lavishly entertaining the vast multitude with all the country afforded. When the time came for the guests to depart for their homes they were loath to go, Kahikikala and Keoua having proved such agreeable and courteous hostess and host. With cordial invitations for renewal of visits and pledges of eternal friendship they took farewell.

Kalokuokamaile had reached his third year a handsome and lovely child, but there was a cloud coming to shadow his bright life. He was soon to lose a kind father's embraces and a parent's unbounded love. An embassy from the long-forgotten father, Keeaumokunui, desired the return of his son Keoua to his paternal home, to accomplish the heart's wish of his parents that he should espouse his cousin Kekuiapoiwa the Second, their niece, they having been betrothed from infancy. Keoua turned to his faithful and downhearted wife, entreating, "What shall I do?"

"Return to your home and obey the desire of your parents and people," in self-sacrificing spirit she replied. "Here is your son, the love of your youth. He will be my comfort and solace, to requite my affection for you in your absence."

The prince bowed low and embraced Kahikikala, saying, "I will do as you bid me."

When preparations were completed for his return to his ancestral home, there was sorrow and weeping all over Hana, for Keoua had endeared himself to the whole country of Hana, Kipahulu and Kaupo. On the day of his departure Keoua turned to Kahikikala and said: "Be tender and loving toward our son and always teach him to understand that it is to obey the dictate of my conscience that I return to my father, for he showed me great love by granting me the great wish of my life to come here in search of you. Although my footsteps are turned homeward, my heart remains with you and our child. With our child I leave my tabu "a noho kane hele ka wahine."

Thus saying he departed; embarking in his canoe, regally fitted up to bear the royal scion home, followed by his suite and attendants.

Part II

In the arrival of Keoua he found his cousin had grown up to be a most agreeable and fascinating woman, and soon the pair had an understanding that not a long courtship would be necessary. Kekuiapoiwa was well pleased with her cousin's looks and manners. As compared with all previous hoaos this one excelled in magnificence, for the two young scions were blood royal of the grand old king Keaweikekahialiiokamoku paternally and maternally in direct line. Everything came off happily and merrily. Every desire of the family had been granted and hopes for the future of the nation were centered in these two young hearts. A few months passed happily with the royal family, a grand and joyous event in the realm being anticipated. The great hope was realized in the birth of their first son, Kamehameha I, destined to become the conqueror of all the islands into one kingdom under his undivided rule. A second son was Kealiimaiai. Two daughters were added to the family, named Peleuli and Piipii. Whether Kekuiapoiwa died without bearing Keoua other than these four children history does not mention, but Keoua formed another matrimonial union, this being with the queen dowager, Princess Kalola of Maui, who was queen consort to King Kaleiopuu of Hawaii, his half-brother. By this union he became the father of Lilihanui, who espoused her first cousin Kiwalao, son of King Kaleiopuu and Queen Kalola.

Kamehameha the First, who became the most noted warrior and eventually conqueror of the whole Hawaiian archipelago, was born at Kohala on the island of Hawaii. He was the second son of Keouakalanikupuapaikalani-nui by his second wife, she being his cousin Kekuiapoiwa.

Although by lineage and blood, both paternally and maternally, this child was considered one of the highest of the high, still the kingship and the crown were in the possession of Kalaninuiamamao, the eldest born of Keaweikekahialiiokamoku, consequently Kalaniopuu at this period ruled over all Kau, Kona and a portion of Kohala; Keawemauhili was the reigning chief of Hilo and Puna, while the region from Mauna Kea to Hualalai and adjacent districts of Waimea was under the rule of the high chief Hinai.

From his infancy Kamehameha always showed signs of bravery and a great desire for athletic contests, spear-wielding, ulu maika, and other magnificent exercises of that period. As he grew to maturity he sought the friendship of his uncle, King Kalaniopuu, becoming a great favorite at the royal court, along with his cousin, Prince Kiwalao, the heir-apparent, whose mother was Princess Kalola of Maui.

King Kalaniopuu had two other sons by different mothers, the second of the family being named Keouakuhauula, and the other Kaoleioku. The latter was by his last queen, Kanekapolei.

Thus far everything apparently was in perfect harmony. But soon the king's health began to fail and, as his demise approached, he called for his courtiers and other dignitaries of the realm to assemble and listen to his proclamation, which ran in this wise:

"I leave all my possessions, with the exception of those heritages which I have already bestowed upon my two other sons, and the kingdom to my eldest born, Kiwalao. My akua, Kukailimoku, I leave to my nephew, Kamehameha."

Kamehameha felt he was slightingly treated, his dissatisfaction growing to indignation, and in relentless spirit he brooded mischief and rebellion against his once adored cousin. Jealousy, envy and hatred took full possession of his soul. Perhaps he never thought of the mystic significance of the name of the idol god bequeathed to him— "Kukailimoku," the word itself meaning "I conquer."

It did not take Kamehameha long to muster up followers in the regions of Kapalilua, Kona and Kohala, with whom he retraced his steps toward Kau, working up strife and animosity as he went along. His main object was to besiege Kiwalao's camp. There was a fierce and bloody struggle. The Kauites held their position firmly and bravely. The two younger brothers still maintained their guard, rendering assistance to their royal brother in every way.

At length there appeared a sign of capitulation in Kamehameha's army. Shortness of food was telling on its strength, for Kona was then suffering from famine. Instead of surrendering, however, the invaders retreated to the heights above Mauna Loa, where hapuu was abundant. Wild pigs abounded there, and yams, ohias and plantains, even the puhala tree, provided sustenance for the lately famished crowd. Moreover, fish ponds were looted and made desolate.

However, this situation could not long continue. Kamehameha hankered for the warpath and back to Kau he must go. Young and vigorous and of grand physique, he had followers of similar caliber. Among his people were the Heulus, ancestors on the maternal side of the late Queen Liliuokalani, who became famous for their courage and skill in warfare. Also there was Kuhaupio, a noted ancestor of Luahine, grandmother of the late Princess Bernice Pauahi Bishop.

Reinvigorated by their rest, they resumed the march toward Kau. Kiwalao was not of stalwart' build and, even before the clash of arms, it was apparent that his strength was failing. Neither side had won a victory when he died.

Upon the death of Kiwalao his brother, Keoua Kuhauula, placed himself at the head of the host opposing Kamehameha. Events showed the belligerent armies evenly matched. Time and time again the Konaites advanced only to be hurled back. For the second time Kamehameha counted his cause as lost. In his despair he summoned to his presence his most favored general, Keaweaheulu, and gave him this order:

"Go to Keoua Kuhauula and tell him that great is my desire to make friends (ike). You are the best one to bear the message, for you are related to his mother, and he will heed your words sooner than anything I could say to him."

Undoubtedly plans were formed right there for the tragedy of treachery about to be related.

Keaweaheulu on arrival at Kau made known his errand. Immediately the news spread to his brother Kaoleioku's quarters, and at once that chief hastened to Keoua's camp.

"Word has reached me," he said to his brother, "that you are about to embark for a voyage to Kona. If such is your plan, of course my duty is to be by your side in whatever you undertake." To which Keoua Kuhauula replied:

"Here is our kinsman Keaweaheulu with good news from the young chief Kamehameha. To ike is the chief desire of the valiant foe. Thereby bloodshed will cease and tranquillity will prevail all over the land. It is time that our dear and loyal people should find rest."

Without loss of time preparations were undertaken for the expedition to Kona and Kawaihae. At the latter place it was expected that Kamehameha would be awaiting Keoua and his retinue. No harsh winds ruffled the seas of Kona, which on this fated occasion maintained their noted placidity. On the morning of the second day the pretty village of Puako was reached. Upon the beach the inhabitants were already waiting to extend a welcome to the two young princes of Kau. A bounteous feast was in preparation fit to tempt appetites less keen than those of guests just ending a sea voyage. Hea-Inoas, meles and dances entertained the vast crowd.

At the conclusion of the feast Keoua Kuhauula made a move to enjoy the cooling breezes from the shores of Kawaihae bay opposite, but, lo and behold, what is that which meets his gaze? A great fleet of canoes, double and single, in warlike array, was massed within two-thirds of the distance from the Kawaihae beach to Puako. In that hostile demonstration he read his doom, and it was there and then he uttered the words of historic import, in the flowery symbolism of Hawaiian diction, casting his eyes heavenward as he spoke:

"The wind clouds are gathering in the heavens for a storm" (makani luna ka hele ino nei ke ao—this being in allusion to the dread scene before him). "But come forward, my comrades, steer the prows of our barks (i mua ka ihu o ka waa) to that fatal shore yonder."

His followers sprang to obey the command of their glorious chief, well aware of their murderous betrayal under the guise of friendship, but as dauntless as their heroic and high-born leader. But where at this moment was Keaweaheulu, the treacherous instrument of this most dastardly foul play? Before Keoua Kuhauula's battle canoe reached the shore, it was attacked and boarded by Kamehameha's warriors. Over-powering Keoua they bound him hand and foot, according to orders, and bore him to the landing place, where he was promptly slain.

In the meantime the prime author of this very foul deed, Kamehameha, looked down upon the proceedings from an eminence beside the entrance of his newly finished heiau, Puu Kohola. This act of Kamehameha was a big blot on his escutcheon. When the body of his late gallant foe was about to be offered solemnly in sacrifice to Kamehameha's god, a movement was made toward furnishing the "moepuu," or companion, in observance of the traditional custom under which the nearest relative of the principal victim should undergo the same fate.

Kaoleioku was pursued and captured, but as he was being led to the scaffold, Kamehameha, the tumult having reached his ears, at the top of his voice shouted his most solemn tabu, "Mamalahoa kanawai:"

"Refrain; no chief even of the highest rank shall endanger the life of my keiki," he proclaimed, referring to Kaoleioku. ("Keiki means an own son, a nephew, a cousin's son, or even a friend's son.) The voice of authority saved the young man's life. It also established Kaoleioku's family thereafter as belonging to the Kamehameha line.

When our gracious and good King Kauikeouli (Kamehameha III) promulgated the first constitution of the Hawaiian kingdom the law of succession was established, it being set forth therein that after him the succession should fall on his nephew and adopted son, Alexander Liholiho, the youngest son of his half-sister, Kinau, one of Kamehameha's own daughters; then, failing an issue, on his elder brother, Lot Kamehameha; and, still failing an issue, the crown should descend to their only sister, Victoria Kamamalu. But fate decreed otherwise. Death claimed the young princess before she could claim the crown of Hawaii.

Yet the line of succession goes no further. Kamehameha III ignored wider claims to the Kamehameha dynasty, when he conferred on the Legislature the right to appoint any alii of the realm, male or female, to be the stirps of a new royal family of Hawaii.

Part III

Liliha and Kiwalao had only one child, a daughter, who was named Keopuolani, who became one of Kamehameha's consorts, the third in the line avowed by the aliis and people alike. His first queen was Kaahumanu, daughter of the great warrior, Keeaumoku Nohonaapeape, and granddaughter of Kekaulike, king of Maui and adjacent islands of Molokai, Lanai, Kahoolawe and Molokini. Kamehameha by his great power and valor was now the Alii Aimoku of all the islands save Kauai, an absolute monarch, and everything he did was looked upon by the chiefs and people as right and lawful. As the young Princess Keopuolani grew up to womanhood there was no adult alii of the male line equal in rank to her and so eligible to become her husband, although a high chief descended from the line of chiefs of Maui and Hawaii royalty, Ulumaheihei Hoapili, was regarded as her spouse. But Hoapili knew the rules of the aliipios and always held her sacred as belonging by right of birth to Kamehameha, acknowledging the supremacy of the king as decreed by the gods of their forefathers. There was the strongest friendship existing between the king and Hoapili, which lasted beyond the grave.

Kamehameha had two sons by Keopuolani, the eldest being Liholiho, who succeeded him as king of the whole group under the title of Kamehameha II, and who unfortunately went to England, as he thought, for the good of his country, but died there together with his queen, Kamamalu. Their bodies were conveyed to the islands by Capt. Lord Byron through instructions of King William IV, then reigning over Great Britain. Liholiho's brother Kauikeouli, who succeeded him on the throne as Kamehameha III, was a minor at his succession and the regency was assumed already by Kinau II, daughter of Kamehameha I by his second queen consort, Kaheiheimalie, one of Queen Kaahumanu's sisters, also a sister of Kamamalu, widow of Kamehameha II. Nahienaena was another of the line by Keopuolani and Kamehameha I, a daughter who died in childbirth having married a high chief of Hawaii named Leleiohoku.

Part IV

Returning to the Kamehameha line, we come next to Kinau, second daughter of the old sovereign by Kaheiheimalie, who became princess regent of the islands. She married first her cousin, Kahalaia, and had one son, but unfortunately both father and son died young. As it was important that in the position she held, that of an alii of highest rank, her line should be increased, she took unto herself an alii descended of an old line of noted warrior kings, Keawehanaui Kawalu, only son of Lonoikamakahiki Kapuokalani and Kaikilanialiiwahine o Puna, the ancestors of Kekuanaoa. Their firstborn was Moses Kekuaiwa, who died early, and their next son was Lot Kamehameha, who succeeded his younger brother, Alexander Liholiho (Kamehameha IV), as King Kamehameha V. Their only sister, Victoria Kamamalu, died during Kamehameha V's reign.

Alexander Liholiho was adopted by his uncle, Kamehameha III, so therefore took precedence on the throne, in the decree made by that king regarding the succession laws of the country. As Kamehameha V and his sister, Victoria Kamamalu, remained single and Kamehameha IV's only child, the Prince of Hawaii (whose mother was Emma Kaleleonalani, the great-granddaughter of Keealiimaikai, Kamehameha I's brother), died very young, the throne was left void of heirs. Hence the hereditary sovereignty enjoyed by this illustrious royal family of the famous line of the Kamehamehas ceased with Kamehameha V's death, and the country now was to pass on under the constitutional laws created and enacted by Kamehameha III, with the legislature of his time, whereby the sovereignty of the islands after the passing of the Kamehamehas should be an elected monarchy.

Part V

The fourth of the line of Keoua's wives was Kamakaehikuli. She bore him a son named Kaleimamahu, who married Kaheiheimalie and had a daughter named Kekauluohi, mother of King Lunalilo. No sooner than news of the death of Kamehameha V had reached all parts of the islands William Lunalilo was acclaimed as the choice of the people, from Hawaii to Niihau.

Prince William Lunalilo, being a member of the royal house of Keoua by his mother Kekauluohi, was the most favored choice of the whole nation, to await the final approval of the Legislature, and he ascended the throne with the brightest prospects for a happy and prosperous reign.

But the people were doomed to encounter a bitter disappointment soon afterward, for his death took place a little more than a year after he ascended the throne of Hawaii. He left the whole of his property for the care and maintenance of indigent Hawaiians. The interregnum which occurred was of a most excitable nature. Two claimants to the throne—Queen Dowager Emma, widow of Kamehameha IV, and the high chief, David Kalakaua, were backed by two different factions. Kalakaua was descended on his father's side from the royal line of Kalaninuiamamao, the firstborn son of Keaweikekahialiiokamoku and elder brother of Keeaumokunui, father of Keoua Kalanikupuapaikalaninui.

Kalakaua won the day, bringing the rule of the Kalaninuiamamao family, and was enthroned as king of the Hawaiian Islands.

The case was very promising for the future safety of the throne as to a line of succession, for Kalakaua already had two married sisters and a young brother of twenty years, besides a little niece of five or six years, as heirs apparent or presumptive. Kalakaua, empowered by law to nominate his successor, proclaimed his brother Leleiohoku as heir-apparent. The All-wise Creator willed it otherwise. In the full glory of his expanding manhood the young man lost his life through an epidemic then raging in town. Two or three years later the younger of the two sisters died and the elder sister, who had already been proclaimed as the heir apparent, and the young niece were left as the only members of the Kalakaua dynasty in the line of succession. Upon the death of Kalakaua, or when the event first became known in Honolulu by the arrival of his body from San Francisco in the U. S. S. "Charleston" in 1891, Princess Liliuokalani, the heir apparent and regent during his ill-fated visit to California, succeeded him but was dethroned by revolution on January 17, 1893.

Princess Kaiulani, who had been heir presumptive up to that event, was put forward by some friends as a candidate for the throne if restoration of the monarchy should be accepted as the solution of unsettled conditions of the government, but an unsuccessful uprising on behalf of Liliuokalani in January, 1895, ended all the hopes of Hawaiian royalty, and about four years later the beloved young princess, after her country had been annexed to the United States, died in Honolulu from the effects of a cold that she had contracted while on a visit to Hilo. Queen Liliuokalani lived in dignified retirement for nearly a quarter of a century after the overthrow of the monarchy by revolution.

Part VI

K ealiimaikai took to wife the high chiefess Kalikookalani of the Kalaninuiamamao line. They had an only daughter whom they named Kaoanaeha, described by old historians as strikingly handsome. Just about this time there arrived at the port of Kailua, Hawaii, two of England's sons, pioneers, who had come to cast their lot among the aborigines of these isles of the Pacific. Their presence raised quite a commotion and when the news reached King Kamehameha he immediately sent one of his bodyguards to extend to them the hand of welcome with a message that it was his majesty's pleasure to meet the young strangers and offer them a home near his own. It was an unlooked-for happiness.

These young men, by name John Young and Isaac Davis, became great favorites of the king, especially when he had become apprised of the fact that they were experts in the handling of firearms, the use of which was unknown in Hawaii at that period. The day was fast approaching when the fate of two young people would be a matter of great importance.

Kaoanaeha was a girl of fourteen or fifteen summers when she first met her destined husband at her uncle's court. John Young was of fine physique and noble bearing. It was noticed by those around that the two were mutually impressed with the society of one another, so when the question of their marriage was proposed by the king it touched their hearts' greatest desire and met their prompt assent.

Our old marriage custom was a great novelty to the Britisher. I have no doubt that he was cognizant of the honor bestowed on him, and realized that his position would bring him in close touch with royalty. After the usual pomp and gaiety which accompanied those occasions they became man and wife. Kamehameha made them presents of lands for their home and estate. Three beautiful daughters and a son graced the Young home in after years. The son occupied the high office of premier in the latter part of Kamehameha III's, and the fore part of Kamehameha IV's reign. Fanny Kekela II, the elder daughter, who espoused a high chief named Naea, became the mother of Emma Kaleleonalani, queen consort of Kamehameha IV. One of the younger daughters was mother of Peter Young Kaeo and his brother Prince Albert Kunuiakea.

Along with Young's initiation into royalty, Isaac Davis, his bosom friend, was also admitted to the ranks of Hawaiian nobility. He gained the sanction of the sovereign to wed a Hawaiian lady of rank. They had two daughters and a son. The elder daughter became the wife of an Englishman of later arrival, Captain Adams, owner of valuable properties in Honolulu and adjacent districts. Her sister was married into the royal family of Kauai, but unfortunately died without issue. Hueu, the son, married the high chiefess Kaanapilo of the Waimea line of chiefs, who raised a large family of eight sons and daughters, from which Miss Lucy Peabody and her niece, Mrs. Edgar Henriques, are descended.

So the adventures of these enterprising Englishmen ensued not only in distinction and affluence for themselves, but in highest positions for some of their posterity—notably, one as Queen Emma of revered memory, and another as daughter-in-law of a king.

The elder sister of Kamehameha, Peleuli, was grandmother of the high chiefess Kekauonohi through her only son and child, Kinau. Kekauonohi married first Kealiiahonui, the eldest son of Kaumualii, king of Kauai, by whom there was no issue. Secondly, she married Haalelea, a relative of Queen Dowager Kalama, consort of Kamehameha III, who was also childless. The youngest of Kekuiapoiwa's children was named Piipii. She had an only son by name Kanihonui ("big teeth").

Keoua's last matrimonial venture was to marry Akahi, the companion of his old age, a chiefess who became the mother of Kaleiwohi, who took to wife Kailipakalua. Their son Pauwelua married Kaluai of the Waimea, Hawaii, line of chiefs, and begot the late chiefess Akahi, who became the wife of Keeaumoku the second, Queen Kaahumanu's younger brother, second cousin of Mrs. Kekaaniau Pratt and third cousin of Mrs. Bernice Pauahi Bishop.

Probably the matrimonial enterprises of Keoua were carried through in observance of the rule of creating pios after the example of his forefathers, making him in duty and honor bound to promote the line of inheritance along varied branches.

Part VII

N ow to return to the first memoirs of this narrative, we shall speak of Kalokuokamaile, the first offspring of Keoua, whom we left as a child. Years have passed by and Kalokuokamaile has grown up a strong, athletic man, of good and mild nature, with no selfish or ambitious motives. His single aim was to secure the happiness and contentment of his people. His mother had died and now he was the ruler of the kingdom in her stead. He had already taken a wife from the neighboring district of Kahikinui and Honuaula, ruled over by a chief family of which Kaloiokalani was the only flower. Tidings of her fine qualities had reached Hana. Kalokuokamaile set out to visit that court. Of course he had to observe the tabu of his family, paying his visits by night. He was happily received by the parents and soon arrangements for the royal nuptials were completed. When the hoao had taken place and feasting and dancing ended, Kalokuokamaile made preparations to return to Hana. As Kaloiokalani was a great favorite with her people, they volunteered to get up a great cavalcade to escort the distinguished couple as far as Kipahulu. It was said at the time that, so immense was the throng, the procession was mistaken for an invasion by some unknown enemy. However, Kalokuokamaile was at last settled at the old family homestead and affairs ran smoothly and lovely. A bright little girl soon appeared on the scene. They named her Kaohelelani, and she was fated to be their only child. She was verging into maidenhood when Kalokuokamaile died. His people showed their affectionate regard for him by making his grave on the highest peak of their country, Kauwiki. Upon news of his death reaching Kamehameha I he immediately assembled a retinue of followers and retainers to accompany his brother Kealiimaikai to bear his request to Kaloiokalani to permit her daughter Kaohele to take up her residence at his court, and to have his brother take charge of the vast patrimonial estate until Kaohele should reach her majority. This request was granted, for how could a weak woman go contrary to the wish of a powerful chief, as Kamehameha had grown to be, having by this time subjugated all the islands. As Kaohele approached maturity Kamehameha was looking around to obtain a matrimonial alliance for his fair niece. As the Waimea people, under the rule of their high chief Hinai, had shown reluctance to submit to the sway of the great conqueror, Kamehameha took the mild course of uniting the ruling families through an offer of the hand of Kaohele to Nuhi, the eldest son of Hinai. The offer was accepted and soon Kachele was transported to her new home with becoming grace.

The bait had taken its prey but King Kamehameha was sorely disappointed in his expectations. Kaohele became so attached to her new home and relatives, and contented with them, that the anticipated intimacy between the two families was not realized. Or, possibly, she felt resentment toward her august relative owing to what happened to her old beloved home, for, after Kamehameha had conquered the Maui king, he began to partition out, to the chiefs who had aided him, the land that was the rightful heritage of his niece. Whatever disillusions she may have suffered, however, she bore in silence.

There were born to Nuhi and Kaohele first a daughter and then a son, the girl being named Kekaikuihala and the boy Laanui. Kamehameha, although fierce and cruel in war, was disposed to be conciliatory toward those he conquered, aiming to make amends in a measure for the wrongs he inflicted and to establish friendly relations with families to which he had brought misfortune. He extended a welcoming hand and opened his heart to many, men and women alike, who flocked to his hospitable court. Alliances in this way were created, and one by one new homes spread over the lately deserted countryside once more, through the influence of which contentment was made to rule supreme in the land.

Among the visitors to the royal court was Kekuwai-Piia, who had just become a widow, coming as a guest of her sister, Queen Kaahumanu. Laanui was a boy growing to maturity. The king had not forgotten the great wish of his heart, coveting possession of Waimea and hoping to gain it, if not in battle, through a matrimonial alliance. His failure to accomplish this end through Kaohele was a sting to the old warrior's pride, and now he chose a new agent of his ambition by inviting Laanui to the court. The invitation was gladly accepted and the visit lasted for months. Kamehameha was loath to have Laanui depart while he was slyly intriguing with Kaahumanu to negotiate a marriage between Piia and Laanui. Piia is described as being a person heavily built and not prepossessing in appearance like her sisters Kaahumanu and Kaheiheimalie. When at last the proposition was put squarely to Laanui, that it was the united wish of the king and queen that the marriage should take place, for a moment he was dejected. To wed a woman very many years his senior was not the desire of his heart. Yet realizing that it might be perilous to go contrary to the express desire of the powerful monarch he quietly consented "to take the bitter pill."

The couple took up their residence at Waialua, permanently, upon one of the divisions of land which Piia had received as her portion out of her father's large estate. Soon afterward the old conqueror's death occurred, upon which Kaahumanu became regent of the whole group. The first party of missionaries had just arrived. Piia and Laanui, together with Queen Kaahumanu and several other chiefly persons, were among the first converts to Christianity. Likewise Laanui and Piia were one of the first couples to be married by Mr. Bingham. Their favorite dwelling was at Waialua, Island of Oahu. They found the climate there so salubrious and balmy that they loved it, visiting Honolulu only when their presence at court was demanded. Unfortunately her corpulence did not inure to healthfulness and before long Piia sickened and died. Before passing away she said to her husband: "Laanui, I wish to divulge a secret in my heart to you. It was not my work that you gave up your patrimonial inheritance to me. It was at the instigation of Kamehameha that I played coyly toward you in order to gratify his selfish motives. For your cheerful sacrifice of what was so dear to your heart I feel it is my duty to repay you. Therefore in return for great kindness I leave this dear Waialua to you, as well as all the other lands which I own, for my token of love for you. I cannot die happy without making this reparation while the breath is in my body. Forgive me for the part I took in the wrongful measure."

Laanui, in the presence of their large retinue of friends, relatives and retainers, pronounced the desired forgiveness. A few days later Piia was no more.

Part VIII

In Queen Kaahumanu's court there were two little girls whom she had taken to bring up, twins, daughters of the pioneer Frenchman, Mons. Jasson Rives (whose Hawaiian name designated by Queen Kaahumanu was Luahine), who had landed on these shores and become the Aikane-Punahele of Prince Liholiho, the heir apparent to the throne. He had taken to wife Holau II, a descendant of Kaihikapumahana, the only daughter of Lonoikamakahiki Kapuokalani and his wife Kaikilanialiiwahine o Puna and sister of Keawehanauikawalu, ancestor of Kekuanaoa, father of the last line of the Kamehamehas. Mrs. Judd spoke of the twin girls as becomingly pretty. As they grew up they were greatly sought after in marriage and Virginia Kahoa was the first to leave their adopted home. She became the wife of Mr. Henry Aucurs Peirce, one of the rich merchants among such as Brewer and Hunnewell, Ladd & Co., and a few others. Subsequently Laanui found in the elder sister, Teresa Owana Kaheiheimalie the choice of his heart and his second wife. He was then almost twice the age of his young wife but that did not mar the match, for his gentleness and kindly disposition had completely won her affection. They lived at Waialua most of the time. Their town residence is now owned by the James Campbell estate, its frontage being on Punchbowl, Hotel and Likelike streets, just above the Library of Hawaii. In time a little daughter appeared on the scene to bless their union and the people from all around Waialua visited the new-born babe with a hookupu in silver dollars. That custom was styled "palala." No one could have a view of the little stranger unless they came with their "mohai" in their hands. Friends and interested people from Honolulu also brought offerings to mingle with those of Waialua and were generously entertained by Laanui and Owana.

They named their darling child Elizabeth Kekaaniauokalani—"Elizabeth" after the baptismal name of Queen Kaahumanu and the Hawaiian name after one of Laanui's sisters, the firstborn of the family, who died at the age of five years. Elizabeth was idolized by her parents and the people of Waialua living under Laanui. For five years they longingly hoped for a male heir further to brighten their home before their wish was realized. They named their little son Gideon (after the father) and Kailipalaki o Keheananui (after the high alii Kinau II). It became evident soon after the birth of their little son that Owana's health was failing. Dr. Judd, the resident physician and one of the missionaries, did all in his power to save the afflicted mother, but in two months grief over a departed wife for the second time was Laanui's portion.

Part IX

It was at this time that Kauikeouli, Kamehameha III, was seriously consulting with his chiefs about establishing a select school for the children of royal and chiefly families.

The site was already provided by the king, being on the lot where the old barracks now stands. It took more than a year to construct the building, which was one of adobe of the old Spanish style, a square edifice enclosing a central court. With the assistance of Dr. Judd the choice of teachers and a general manager was made, Mr. Amos S. Cooke and his wife, of the missionary colony, being the first ones in charge of the institution. It was made a boarding school so that the teachers would have the immediate and full control of the pupils.

Seven boys and seven girls were selected from the highest chief families in the realm. The boys were the three sons of Kinau and Kekuanaoa—Moses Kekuaiwa, Lot Kamehameha, and Alexander Liholiho; William Lunalilo, son of Kekauluohi and Kanaina; James Kaliokalani and David Kalakaua, sons of Kapaakea and Keohokalole, and Peter Young, son of Kaeo and Lahilahi. The girls were Jane Loeau and Abigail Maheha, daughters of Liliha III and her husband Namaile; Bernice Pauahi, daughter of Konia and Paki; Emma Rooke, daughter of Kekela and Naea; Lydia Kamakaeha, daughter of Kapaakea and Keohokalole; Victoria Kamamalu, daughter of Kinau and Kekuanaoa, and Elizabeth Kekaaniau, daughter of Laanui and Owana.

As Victoria Kamamalu was only two years old at the opening of the school, it was deemed necessary that her "kahus," John Ii and Sarai his wife, should attend her in school residence. The tuition was principally in English. From time to time the Cookes required assistant teachers. French and Spanish tutors were also introduced, the older scholars forming their classes.

For ten years the Royal School continued according to the original design, but the great responsibility was beginning to tell on the health of our dear instructor. Mr. Cooke was compelled to seek an entire change and rest. Most of us left for our own homes but still attended the school. The tuition was taken up by a Mr. Fuller, who had already started a school of his own with children from some of the most respectable families, foreign and Hawaiian, resident in Honolulu. Then the name of

Honolulu Academy was given to the school, which, however, continued only for a short time.

When Mr. Fuller gave up teaching, the Government, with Mr. Richard Armstrong as Minister of Instruction, started to build the later Royal School (supplanted a few years ago by the present modern edifice), thinking it most appropriate to name it such since Victoria Kamamalu, Liliuokalani and a few other children of chiefs of a younger generation had not as yet finished their education. Mr. George Beckwith, Mr. Armstrong's son-in-law, was put in as instructor of that school, and all the pupils that had attended the old academy were admitted to it.

In forming the old genuine Royal School, the future positions of some of the pupils were already decided. Moses and Lot were respectively to hold the governorships of Kauai and Maui. Victoria, who had been betrothed in infancy to William Lunalilo, was to hold the premiership third in line from her mother Kinau, and Lunalilo as her husband would fill the office of governor of Oahu after Kekuanaoa's death. Alexander Liholiho was already regarded as heir presumptive to the throne, for Kamehameha III had lost his only son in infancy. The governorship of the Island of Hawaii lay in abeyance for future nomination.

Undoubtedly our parents had their own secret plans and expectations regarding all our futures, but, truth to tell, among that princely throng only one of the supposedly well-laid schemes was carried out. This singular instance not only gladdened the hearts of the parents concerned but of the community at large, being no less than the marriage of King Kamehameha IV and the High Chiefess Emma Rooke. The others formed alliances with other chief families and prominent American families that had decided to make their homes in this happy land, the "Paradise of the Pacific."

But it is sad to relate that out of that most promising group of youthful scions of Hawaii's nobility—descendants of the royal houses of Keaweikekahialiiokamoku of Hawaii, the Piilanis and Kamalalawalus of Maui, the Kakuihewas and Kaleiomanuias of Oahu and the Manokalanipos of Kauai—there remains but one survivor to cherish the reminiscences of those dear, sweet days of long ago, and that one the writer of this small literary souvenir of Hawaii's most palmy times.

Part X

When the death of our dear father occurred at his favorite home at Waialua, I was still a minor and attending school as such. We were fortunate to have still living some members of our mother's family, her twin sister and two brothers, who grasped the occasion to claim their right to take me to their home and protection. Before this could be arranged notice had to be given to the king and chiefs that, owing to failing health, Mr. Cooke with his family was going to change his residence from the school to the mission neighborhood.

Eventually a guardian was appointed in the person of John Ii, a justice of the supreme court, who was also administrator of my father's estate. Upon arriving at maturity I was advised to claim my portion of my father's estate. When I called on my guardian for this purpose, he astounded me with the information, "There is not much property that I know of which belonged to your father."

Being young and unsuspicious I turned toward home little suspecting the wrongs inflicted on myself and brother. How we had been wronged remained a mystery until several years afterward, when a very confidential retainer of my father's took sick and, fearing that death might overtake him at any moment, despatched a boy to our home in town urging me to come to his bedside, as he wished to see me once more before the end came.

Early next morning, in company with one of my uncles and accompanied by Kuokoa's boy, I rode post-haste to Waialua, reaching there about 4 or 5 o'clock in the afternoon. We found the old gentleman awaiting our arrival in great anxiety. After we had partaken of some food the household was summoned to evening prayers as usual, by the sick man's couch, and after delivering the blessing of God he turned and addressed me thus:

"My dear young Alii, I have been a traitor to you and your cause. I have been false to my haku, your beloved father, who brought us to this new residence aside from our own loved land of Waimea, the birthplace of your dear father and his ancestors before him. He placed in my hands a book, which you will find in your room, containing a list of lands to be presented to the Land Office just newly created to secure the legal award of title as ordained by law. I did not follow your father's command, but listened to the tempter."

ELIZABETH KEKAʻANIAU LAʻANUI PRATT

Such were the words he spoke before a dozen of us who had congregated before him. And furthermore he said, "All the lands that I possess as presents from your father it is my wish that they be returned to you after the death of my wife."

Little did we suppose that those words would be his last. About 2 o'clock that night we were aroused from deep slumber with wailing from his room. Life had fled. We remained for two days after the funeral of Kuokoa, then, with John Ii and our party, started homeward bound to our dear old Honolulu.

For years my father's old devoted kahus remained and watched over the loved spot where once my father dwelt. Nothing could induce them to sever the tie binding them to the place they cherished for the sake of their lamented master. But there came a change.

One of his people who lived in the Koolau district, by name Kuaea, was invited by the people of Waialua to become the pastor of the old Hawaiian church there. Upon application to me for permission to live on the old homestead, arrangements were immediately made to build him a nice home. His flowing speech and pleasant delivery won the hearts of his congregation and his popularity became famous. It extended to Honolulu and, with a larger salary offered him by the old Kaumakapili Church, he was induced to change his residence to the metropolis. He gave up the house that he had built on my premises as a token of thankfulness.

Then it was that my interest in Waialua began to awaken. Years and experience had grown on me. We required a country residence and, with the kind help of my husband, made many improvements on our small holding which had been long neglected. I found the climate of my childhood's home (for I first saw the light there) far excelled in salubrity any other place on the Island of Oahu. What with the delicious bathing in the placid waters of Anahulu flowing past our door (where now the stately and popular Haleiwa Hotel stands), many a happy hour was spent with women and children swimming around one in joyous glee.

I must confess that I was loath to take my leave of that sylvan-like spot to assume the cares and responsibilities awaiting me in town. No wonder it had such a hold upon my dear father's life.

Years and experience! Yes. People to whom my father had entrusted lands of his came to me giving information such as that Kamakau for one lived on the land of Waihee, East Maui, knowing no other lord over him but Laanui, who held sway over other places in the district of

Hana. Kapena's brother was another, holding lands at Lahaina. Laanui, a namesake of my father, was put in charge of the Kapapala land (now in possession of Mr. Julian Monsarrat). Many other properties might be mentioned, among them the Panalaau land of Eleele on Kauai, which my father received as his bounty for taking sides with Kamehameha against Kaumualii, king of Kauai. This land my father had entrusted to the care of one of his retainers named Wahineaea, a relative of Kuokoa.

But what recompense have they rendered to the children of Laanui? Nothing, but robbery from first to last. Not one inch of ground was marked to denote that once it belonged to Laanui, their kind friend and benefactor.

Waialua, as you have seen and read, was honestly acquired by Laanui, not only in exchange for his patrimonial estate of Waimea by intrigue and cunning on the part of that greedy despot, Kamehameha, but by virtue of sincere love and affection from his wife Piia. Who are the owners of that fair land now? Bishop Estate everywhere, as one of Victoria's possessions. Thank God we have outlived those days of misery and bitterness.

It was on the appeal of my aunt, who said we had enough to live on, that I refrained from starting litigation for the recovery of our rightful inheritance.

Part XI

Thus we see Keoua Kalani Kupuapaikalaninui as the progenitor not only of the Keoua line but likewise of the Kamehamehas. Gideon Kailipalaki Laanui by his wife Kamaikaopa left an only child, a daughter, Teresa Owana Kaohelelani, who, by her late husbands, A. J. Cartwright, Junior, and the Hon. Robert W. Wilcox, has a family of children and grandchildren, forming the junior branch of the Keoua family, now living. They, with the writer of these memoirs as the only sole representative of the senior line, comprise the only descendants of the grand and famous chieftain, whose history we are about to close.

Before concluding and to give the readers some idea of what the ancient "Meles" are, a sample out of many is given here which was sung to Keoua Kalanikupuapaiakalani Nui while living, and handed down from generation to generation until inherited by the present owner, the writer of this book. These meles not only recite the genealogical line of the family, but also describe great events of the time to which they relate:

He Koi Honua

O ke Kupa ai ka lani, o Keawe ke 'Lii,
Ka Okala, Onu, paka ai ka lani,
O ka Lani hoi ke Lii ku-ka-ea,
Ku-ka-ea, ka hili honua o na Lii,
Ahu kupanaha o na Lii ilaila,
Holoi ka Lena, ka paa o Kukailani,
Nani Umi a Umi Kukailani,
Na puko ula a Makakaualii,
Ka Akia, Auhuhu, Awahia, Mulea,
E pualena ai ke kai,
Lena koko kapu o Iwikauikaua,
Holo ka ahihi a Keakealani,
Auamo, ahai, Keawe iaia,
Huna aku la i ka wekiu o ka Lani,
Kau aku i luna i ka Haka kau Alii,
Noho i ka nuu, i ka Haka-Nuu-Lani,
He Lani Nuu-nuu, he opeope kapu,
He opeope, he kaa ai kino no Keawe,

O hookino a moa, o Keaweikekahialiiokamoku,
Mau-mau mai Keawe me he pa ai la,
O ka lihi oi Keawe, o Kauhi ke aka,
Pono no i Kuamoo o Haloa,
Ku i ka Naho i ka Nahawele na Lii,
He kena-kena, awahia ka lani o Umi,
Ka-hau-ana no ka Lani ka-hau,
He kulike ana no ka Lani ku like,
He liu-liu *he kaawale na Lii nui,*
Ka Poho-ula ai o Makua ke Kupuna,
Ke kaheka kai e miko ai ka waha,
Mikomiko *ka lehelehe o I ke kupuna,*
Puhalau oo *i Ahu a I,*
Ka Puniu kaukahi o I kanaka
Lea wale ia Hula, o Imaikalani,
I ka hauna hema no a Imaikalani,
Kukai ka Ila o Puapuakea,
Kanaloa aku, a haahaa ilalo,
Uu ae, ho ae iluna,
Hana ka laau o Wawakailani,
Pa i ka ai o ka hua lepo,
Newa i ka luahi o Makakuikalani,
Ka Luahi Nui Makaakaa he Lii,
He Lii i loko o ka huku maia kapu,
Ke ea malaiula o Kahai ka ua lau,
O ka lele maia i Humuula,
Ka lila maia io ole,
He ai *na Papa me Wakea,*
He ai kapu *kike io ia nei,*
Elima i mua, elima i ka wahine,
He mau alii hua Lala Kama-hele
He Kamahele ka lani, he nioi ke Lii,
E o ke Alii nona ia Inoa,
O Kekaaniauokalani he inoa—
E—o—e—

Kalanikupuapa-i-kalani Nui Keoua lived to a good old age. His remains now repose in one of those natural vaults or caves on the heights of the cliffs overlooking Kealakekua Bay.

Written by his great-great-grand daughter, the High Chiefess Elizabeth Kekaaniauokalani Kalaninuiohilaukapu Pratt.

THE END

A Note About the Author

Elizabeth Keka'aniau La'anui Pratt (1834–1928) was a Hawaiian high chiefess and historian. Born in Waialua, she was named after Queen Ka'ahumanu, her grandmother by adoption, whose baptized name was Elizabeth. Raised in the inner circle of Kamehameha I, Elizabeth was educated at the Chiefs' Children's School, where five of her sixteen classmates would go on to serve as monarchs of the Kingdom of Hawaii. A close friend of Emma, queen consort of Kamehameha IV, she eventually served as her lady in waiting and was active in the royal court. In 1864, she married Franklin Seaver Pratt, an American businessman and naturalized citizen of the kingdom. A lifelong ally of Queen Emma, Elizabeth supported her failed candidacy for the royal election of 1874, which led to rioting after popular support for the Queen was ignored by the assembly gathered at Honolulu Courthouse. During the period of political unrest preceding the overthrow of the Kingdom of Hawaii, the Pratts moved briefly to San Francisco, where Franklin acted as Hawaiian Consul General in the Pacific states. Toward the end of her life, she participated in numerous ceremonies to honor the history of the Hawaiian Kingdom, and in 1920 wrote her History of Keoua Kalanikupuapa-i-kalani-nui, Father of Hawaiian Kings, a genealogical study of the House of Keōua Nui.

A Note from the Publisher

Spanning many genres, from non-fiction essays to literature classics to children's books and lyric poetry, Mint Edition books showcase the master works of our time in a modern new package. The text is freshly typeset, is clean and easy to read, and features a new note about the author in each volume. Many books also include exclusive new introductory material. Every book boasts a striking new cover, which makes it as appropriate for collecting as it is for gift giving. Mint Edition books are only printed when a reader orders them, so natural resources are not wasted. We're proud that our books are never manufactured in excess and exist only in the exact quantity they need to be read and enjoyed.

bookfinity™

Discover more of your favorite classics with Bookfinity™.

- Track your reading with custom book lists.
- Get great book recommendations for your personalized Reader Type.
- Add reviews for your favorite books.
- AND MUCH MORE!

Visit **bookfinity.com** and take the fun Reader Type quiz to get started.

Enjoy our classic and modern companion pairings!